Henry Knox

BOOKSELLER, SOLDIER, PATRIOT

BY ANITA SILVEY

PAINTINGS BY WENDELL MINOR

CLARION BOOKS

Houghton Mifflin Harcourt • Boston • New York • 2010

CLARION BOOKS

215 Park Avenue South

New York, New York 10003

Clarion Books is an imprint of Houghton Mifflin Harcourt Publishing Company.

www.hmhbooks.com

The text of this book is set in Grit Primer.

The illustrations are acrylic on gessoed wood panels.

LIBRARY OF CONGRESS CATALOGING-IN-PUBLICATION DATA

Silvey, Anita.

Henry Knox : bookseller, soldier, patriot / by Anita Silvey ; pictures by Wendell Minor.

p. cm.   ISBN 978-0-618-27485-7

1. Knox, Henry, 1750–1806—Juvenile literature. 2. Generals—United States—Biography—Juvenile literature.

3. United States—History—Revolution, 1775–1783—Artillery operations—Juvenile literature.

4. Boston (Mass.)—History—Siege, 1775–1776—Juvenile literature. I. Minor, Wendell. II. Title.   E207.K74S56 2010

355.0092—dc22   [B]   2009045353

Manufactured in Singapore

TWP 10 9 8 7 6 5 4 3 2 1

4500226785

For Dinah Stevenson

—*dear friend and brilliant editor*

A.S.

For Anita

W.M.

CONTENTS

1. A Very Young Bookseller

*W*hen other boys walked, Henry Knox bounced. Where others saw problems, he found possibilities.

In 1750 Henry was born into a working-class Boston family, the seventh of ten sons. His father, a ship captain, carried on trade with the West Indies. But then William Knox failed in business and left his family. At the age of nine Henry quit his studies so that he could help support his mother and siblings.

Although it was difficult for such a young boy to find full-time work, Henry managed to become a bookseller's assistant, at the firm of Wharton and Bowes in Boston. At night Henry read his way through the merchandise—Plutarch's *Lives,* Greek and Roman classics in translation, books on the French language. He particularly enjoyed reading about engineering science and military history.

2. Learning to Be a Soldier

In his teenage years Henry had three main passions. He loved books; he loved cannons and other artillery; and he loved food, all kinds of food. Big boned and broad shouldered, Henry grew to be six feet tall and to weigh around 250 pounds.

Once Henry devoted himself to a cause, he gave himself to it wholeheartedly. Henry not only wanted to read about cannons, but also yearned to use them. For the protection of all the citizens, towns like Boston maintained local companies of soldiers, the local militia. Henry joined one of these groups, called the Train, made up of mechanics and shopkeepers from the South End. During the winter of 1766, British artillery officers, on their way to Quebec, drilled the company.

From these officers Henry learned valuable information about handling small artillery. He practiced on the 3-pound cannon (called this because it shot 3-pound cannon balls). Ten years later, during the American Revolution, he actually used two of the cannons he had been trained on against the British themselves.

3. THE BOSTON MASSACRE

In 1770 about sixteen thousand people lived in Boston, one of the largest cities in America. Because the citizens objected to what they saw as unfair taxing by the British, England sent soldiers to keep the peace.

Small fights between the citizens and the British troops had been occurring for several months. On March 5, 1770, while returning from seeing friends, Henry came upon an angry mob by the Custom House on King Street. The Bostonians had armed themselves with shovels. Yelling "Drive out the lobster-backs!" and "Hang the redcoats," they hurled snow, ice, and other debris at the British soldiers in their bright red uniforms.

Henry implored the officer in command, Captain Preston, to withdraw. "Take your men back. If they fire, your life must answer for the consequences!" Henry shouted.

Then a townsperson struck a soldier with a club, and the British soldiers fired on the crowd. Five Boston men were killed in the fracas that followed, which the local press called the Boston Massacre.

Like most Bostonians, Henry blamed the British for these deaths.

4. LONDON BOOK STORE

*I*n July 1771, when he turned twenty-one, Henry opened the London Book Store in Boston. He paid particular attention to books on military science. Since several thousand British troops and officers now blanketed the streets of Boston, Henry ordered the most important and up-to-date volumes about warfare from England. He studied them himself, asked the officers questions, and became an expert on the way the British conducted war.

Henry enjoyed making his customers, even British ones, feel welcome. His bookshop quickly became a fashionable social club, attracting young gentlemen officers and their girlfriends. Charming and personable, with a winning smile, Henry impressed the British with his military knowledge and skill. They even offered him an army commission as a British officer.

But another set of customers visited Henry in his bookstore—men such as Paul Revere, a silversmith, and Nathanael Greene, a blacksmith from Rhode Island. Like these men, Henry embraced a cause that he could not serve if he joined the British army: the right of the American colonies to determine their own fate.

5. Lucy Flucker

*I*n a hunting accident on Noodle's Island in Boston Harbor, Henry lost the third and fourth fingers of his left hand. After that he always covered that part of his hand with a handkerchief. He cut a splendid figure with his wounded hand bound in silk, and attracted the gaze of many young women.

One of these young women visited Henry's bookshop to talk to him about books. Lucy Flucker and Henry also shared a love of food and hearty eating. But she came from a family of Tories, or British sympathizers. Her father, who served as the royal secretary to the Massachusetts colony, opposed the developing relationship between his daughter and Henry. Thomas Flucker felt that Henry Knox backed the wrong cause and worked in a trade, bookselling, that was unlikely to make much money.

But Henry and Lucy had fallen in love. Despite the feelings of Lucy's parents, the two wed in Boston on June 16, 1774. For almost a year after that, Henry continued backing the same cause and engaging in the same trade.

6. THE BATTLES OF LEXINGTON AND CONCORD

On April 19, 1775, the conflict that had been building between the British troops and the citizens of Massachusetts erupted in the towns of Lexington and Concord, ten miles from the city of Boston. British troops encountered a motley group of armed farmers, known as the Minutemen, on Lexington Common. After an exchange of gunfire, eight American soldiers lay dead and ten wounded on the cold spring ground.

Believing that they could no longer live safely in Boston, Henry and Lucy abandoned the bookstore, gathered up a few personal belongings, and prepared to flee the city. In the dark of a moonless night, they got into a carriage and stole through the streets. To make sure that Henry's sword would get through British lines, Lucy concealed it in the silk lining of her petticoats.

After finding a safe home for Lucy in Worcester, Massachusetts, miles away from Boston, Henry began supervising the building of fortifications outside the city.

7. THE OCCUPATION OF BOSTON

*A*fter the battles of Lexington and Concord, the British bedeviled Boston citizens. They cut down the Liberty Tree—a large elm where Bostonians had gathered to protest—and used it for firewood. They burned buildings and churches. They ripped out pulpits and pews from the Old South Meeting House and used the building as a riding stable. Shops were closed, buildings deserted. British troops surrounded the city and permitted no one to enter or leave. Supplies such as vegetables, flour, coffee, and meat could not be brought in. Unable to leave Boston, many people fell sick.

The British, too, were trapped. Militias had come from all over New England to try to help the people of Boston. They positioned themselves around the city, outside the British lines. These American rebels, known as continentals at the time and patriots today, could not, however, engage the British forces for fear of making things even worse for the Bostonians.

On June 14, General George Washington assumed the role of commander in chief of the Continental army and arrived in nearby Cambridge. About three weeks later, Washington examined two fortresses that Henry had built and praised his work. Afterward Henry devoted himself wholeheartedly to a new cause: serving General George Washington and the Continental army.

8. Guns for General Washington

In the middle of November, Washington told Henry that he had been nominated by the Continental Congress to head the army artillery. Henry wryly asked Washington where his artillery might be found, because only a few pieces existed around Boston. Then Henry shared a plan he had concocted to gain cannons.

Six months before, Benedict Arnold, Ethan Allen, and the Green Mountain Boys, a group of Vermonters who banded together to fight the British, had captured a huge cache of these weapons at Fort Ticonderoga in New York. However, the fort was located three hundred miles from Boston. Between the fort and the city lay high ridges and tall mountains, dense forests, large unpopulated areas, and long lakes. Although many had talked about transporting these guns to Boston, no one had been able to figure out a way to do so.

Henry saw these geographical barriers as opportunities, mere problems to be solved. He convinced Washington that once the ground froze, the artillery could be brought to Boston by oxen and sleds.

Henry's enthusiasm for the project proved contagious. Driven by a need to take action, Washington sent Henry on a critical mission—to bring the cannons of Fort Ticonderoga to Boston.

9. FORT TICONDEROGA

*E*ager to complete his assignment, Henry traveled with his younger brother William to Fort Ticonderoga. On December 5, 1775, they arrived at the fort, where Henry selected the best weapons to take to General Washington. According to Henry's diary, he chose fifty-nine pieces, in assorted shapes and sizes, weighing between 100 and 5,500 pounds. With shapes both slender and dumpy, they ranged in length from one foot to eleven feet. Many of these cannons had been handsomely decorated with carved roosters' or lions' heads. The largest shot 24-pound cannon balls.

In the end, Henry decided to transport around 120,000 pounds of these pieces, approximately the weight of a dozen large elephants. As the weather turned inclement, Henry found boats to carry the guns across Lake Champlain—light flat-bottomed boats (bateaux), long flat-bottomed boats (scows), and smaller and lighter canoes made from hollow trees (piraguas).

Some had already dubbed this expedition Knox's Folly, but Henry with his usual optimism actually believed he could get all of these weapons to George Washington in a few weeks.

10. ACROSS LAKE CHAMPLAIN

After Henry had prepared for the journey, his odd-looking fleet began to move across Lake Champlain. Throughout most of the trip, Henry traveled ahead of his caravan, establishing a route and making arrangements. William Knox stayed with the cannons to ensure that they all got across the lake. Occasionally Henry would go back along the line, shouting orders when necessary. He possessed a deep bass voice that sounded like a sea captain in a gale and inspired confidence.

With his boat crews rowing into cold, biting winds, Henry set out for Fort George at the end of the lake, where he would receive the artillery.

Getting the cannons across the lake proved very difficult. Several of the pieces fell into the water and had to be salvaged. Blue lipped and screaming in pain from the cold, men dove into the icy waters to retrieve them. But William Knox managed to keep the convoy together. Finally all the men and all the artillery arrived at Fort George.

11. "A Noble Train of Artillery"

While at Fort George, Henry had located eighty yokes of oxen and forty-two large and exceedingly strong wooden sleds. He found hundreds of human volunteers to help—frontier traders, teamsters (drivers), timber men, carpenters, blacksmiths, and merchants. He directed the loading of the cannons and settled the weight that each animal should pull. A 9-pound cannon needed four oxen working together; 18-pound and 24-pound cannons required eight. Henry wrote to George Washington on December 17, promising the commander in chief "a noble train of artillery."

Henry's noble train, in reality a hodgepodge caravan, consisted of sleds attached to wide-horned and slow-footed Randall lineback oxen. Even so, it contained all the working artillery of the Continental army.

12. TRAVELING OVER THE ICE

By Christmas Day, Henry was approaching Saratoga, New York. To make progress, he and his men on horseback had to travel through snowdrifts two feet deep. When the party was ready to leave Saratoga, the horses refused to budge. Eventually, Henry and his men arrived on foot at the home of one Squire Fisher, who gave them fresh horses to get to Albany.

In Albany, Henry made plans for the rest of the journey. Then on New Year's Day, Henry and his men cut holes in the ice at various spots on the Hudson River. Through them, water would pour out over the ice, freeze, and strengthen it so the train of artillery could cross safely.

The men worked cautiously to get the guns across the ice; they moved alongside the oxen, with sharp hatchets in their hands to cut the rope if the cannon or sled broke through the ice.

Still, an 18-pound beauty did fall into the river at Half Moon. Leaving a long-anticipated dinner, Henry set out to retrieve the cannon.

13. "All the Kingdoms of the Earth"

Traveling with his teamster father, twelve-year-old John Becker often felt the dangers of the journey. "The road was dreary, the darkness great, and I anything but comfortable during the morning drive. . . . My imagination peopled every bush with ghosts."

But Henry pressed on, worrying about neither ghosts nor the dreary road. In fact, he commented upon the wonders of the terrain in his diary— breathtaking waterfalls and steep mountains from which he could see "all the kingdoms of the earth."

On January 10, the convoy reached the Berkshire Mountains near present-day Warren, Massachusetts. The sleds inched through a treacherous mountain pass where no roads had ever been built.

Once a large gun came over the crest of a mountain or hill, its descent had to be controlled. Chains, bars, and logs were thrown under the runners of the sleds to keep them moving slowly down the mountain. Often the straining muscles of weary men served as the only brakes on the guns, keeping them from plunging down icy hills. Henry believed it almost a miracle that people with heavy loads could get up and down these rock-covered hills.

14. THE OLD SOW

*D*ay by day, the guns lurched through heavy snows. At one spot in the Berkshires, the layer of snow began to get thinner and thinner, making sled travel almost impossible. Finally, a division of the men refused to go any farther. It took Henry three hours to convince them that they would succeed if they continued, and he agreed to find two extra teams of oxen to help pull the artillery. In relative wilderness, eleven miles from Westfield, Massachusetts, he miraculously located these oxen and kept the cannons moving.

When the caravan finally reached Westfield, people crowded into the road, insistent on examining the guns, for they had never seen any so large. Many tried to guess the weight of the cannons. At the sight of one huge piece, nicknamed the Old Sow, the townspeople cheered and asked for a demonstration. Henry had the men place a charge in the 24-pound cannon and set it off. A deep echo resounded across the hills. Fortunately no sound of the cannon, or of the celebration, reached the ears of the British.

Even though the terrain proved easier from this point on, the ground was soft and the guns sank in, so the entourage moved slowly to Springfield. When the party arrived in Framingham, Massachusetts, on January 24, 1776, Henry traveled ahead to Cambridge to report to General George Washington that his mission had been accomplished.

15. DORCHESTER HEIGHTS

On March 4, 1776, the Continental army put Henry's artillery into action. On this extremely dark night, under the command of General John Thomas, four hundred oxen and two thousand men pushed and prodded the cannons onto Dorchester Heights, hills overlooking Boston Harbor. Fortunately the wind carried the noise away from the British army. At sunrise, Washington walked quietly among the men and asked them to remember the day—the anniversary of the Boston Massacre.

As the light of morning came, the British forces were astounded to see a multitude of cannons and new fortifications on the hilltops. Sir William Howe, the British general, said, "The rebels have done more in one night than my whole army would have done in a month." Such an effort, Howe estimated, must have required at least twelve thousand men! Howe decided that the British had been outmaneuvered; since they could not continue to hold Boston, they should evacuate.

Under a flag of truce, the British army and hundreds of Tories—Lucy Knox's parents among them—boarded ships and set sail from Boston Harbor. Lucy never saw her family again.

16. Entering Boston

On March 17 or 18, 1776, General George Washington rode into Boston. By his side was twenty-five-year-old Henry Knox, the local bookseller who had helped free his neighbors.

Henry discovered that the British had destroyed his bookshop. But now he had a different mission—to build an artillery unit for the patriots, relying at first on the weapons he had brought from Fort Ticonderoga.

Together Henry, who later became a general himself, and George Washington rode on to other cities and towns, as the patriots fought to secure the independence of the American colonies. On Christmas Eve in 1776, when Washington needed to cross the Delaware River to surprise the enemy, he put Henry Knox in command. Henry stayed by Washington's side in all the major battles of the war—Valley Forge, Trenton, Princeton, and Yorktown. Throughout the conflict, Washington relied on Henry for his optimism and his enthusiasm, even when the outcome looked bleak.

As a bookseller, Henry insisted that the cannons of Fort Ticonderoga could be used to liberate Boston. As head of artillery for the Continental army, he always believed that the patriots would win.

Henry—who saw possibilities when others saw problems—was right.

SOURCE NOTES

Page 22. These fifty-nine pieces included brass and iron cannons, brass and iron mortars (portable cannons with short barrels), iron howitzers (relatively short-barreled cannons that shot shells at high angles), and some cohorns (small mortars).

Page 27. "A noble train of artillery" is from a letter from Henry Knox to George Washington, December 17, 1775.

Page 27. In his research for *1776*, David McCullough discovered that Henry Knox used Randall lineback oxen, an unusual breed. Information about them can be found at www.randalllineback.com.

Pages 28-29. Information about traveling over the ice is from John P. Becker's *The Sexagenary*, p. 30.

Page 30. "The road was dreary" is from Becker's *The Sexagenary*, p. 27.

Page 30. "All the kingdoms of the earth" is from Henry Knox's diary.

Page 34. "The rebels have done more in one night" is from North Callahan's *George Washington's General*, p. 58.

Page 36. Most sources list March 17 as the date. But historian David McCullough argues that Artemus Ward came in on March 17 and Washington and Knox on March 18. Information from David McCullough, *1776*, p. 106.

HENRY KNOX CHRONOLOGY

July 25, 1750 • *Born in Boston, Massachusetts, seventh son of William Knox and Mary Campbell Knox*

1762 • *William Knox dies in St. Eustatius in the West Indies*

March 5, 1770 • *Boston Massacre*

December 4, 1770 • *Testifies about the Boston Massacre at the trial of Captain Preston*

July 29, 1771 • *Opens London Book Store in Boston*

December 14, 1771 • *Mary Campbell Knox dies in Boston*

June 16, 1774 • *Marries Lucy Flucker in Boston*

Around April 19, 1775 • *Leaves Boston with his wife, Lucy*

May 10, 1775 • *Ethan Allen and Benedict Arnold capture Fort Ticonderoga*

June 17, 1775 • *Continentals lose the Battle of Bunker Hill*

July 1775 • *Meets General George Washington of Virginia*

November 8, 1775 • *Washington writes to the Continental Congress to request that Henry Knox be appointed head of artillery*

November 16, 1775 • *Washington directs Henry Knox to bring cannons from Ticonderoga to Boston*

November 17, 1775 • *Commissioned colonel of the regiment of the artillery by the Continental Congress*

December 5, 1775 • *Arrives at Fort Ticonderoga; begins preparing artillery to travel to Boston*

March 5, 1776 • *Battle of Dorchester Heights*

March 17, 1776 • *General Howe and the Tories evacuate Boston*

Spring 1776 • *Fortifies Manhattan Island, New York*

December 25, 1776 • *Accompanies General Washington across the Delaware River*

January 1777 • *Trenton-Princeton campaign*

September 1777 • *Battle of Brandywine*

October 4, 1777 • *Battle at Germantown*

June 28, 1778 • *Valley Forge and Battle of Monmouth*

October 17, 1782 • *British General Cornwallis surrenders at Yorktown*

1782–84 • *Commands West Point*

November 25, 1783 • *Last British soldiers evacuate New York*

1785 • *Appointed first secretary of war under the Articles of Confederation; retains title after Constitution is adopted*

September 1793 • *Washington puts Henry Knox in charge of the government during Philadelphia's yellow fever epidemic*

1794 • *Retires to private life at Montpelier, his home in Thomaston, Maine*

October 25, 1806 • *Dies at Montpelier*

1926–27 • *Massachusetts and New York establish the General Knox Highway—with markers from Ticonderoga to Boston.*

Around March 17 every year, the city of Boston declares a holiday to celebrate Evacuation Day, when the British left Boston.

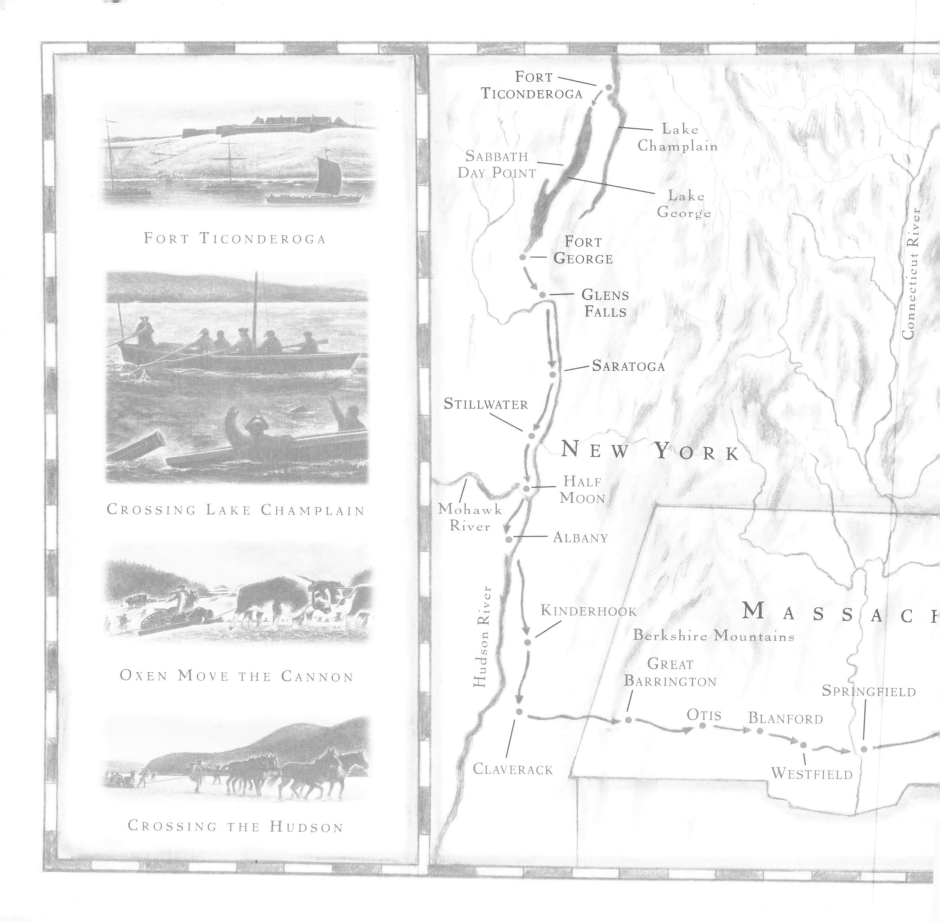

FORT TICONDEROGA

CROSSING LAKE CHAMPLAIN

OXEN MOVE THE CANNON

CROSSING THE HUDSON

FORT
TICONDEROGA

Lake
Champlain

SABBATH
DAY POINT

Lake
George

FORT
GEORGE

GLENS
FALLS

SARATOGA

STILLWATER

NEW YORK

Connecticut River

HALF
MOON

Mohawk
River

ALBANY

Hudson River

KINDERHOOK

Berkshire Mountains

MASSACH

GREAT
BARRINGTON

SPRINGFIELD

OTIS

BLANFORD

CLAVERACK

WESTFIELD